POWE
OF THE
RENEWED
MIND

by

Bill Basansky

Tulsa, Oklahoma

Unless otherwise indicated, all Scripture quotations are taken from the *King James Version* of the Bible.

Power of the Renewed Mind
ISBN 0-89274-021-3

P.O. Box 7126
Fort Myers, Florida 33911

Published by Harrison House, Inc.
P.O. Box 35035
Tulsa, Oklahoma 74153

Printed in the United States of America.

Contents

Foreword

> **And be not conformed to this world: but be ye transformed by the renewing of your mind, that ye may prove what is that good, and acceptable, and perfect, will of God.**
>
> **Romans 12:2**

This verse says that we should be in control of our thoughts and know the difference between good and evil thoughts by testing the spirits.

Remember this: If your thoughts are not entreating, edifying or comforting, they are not of God.

> **For God has not given us the spirit of fear; but of *power*, and of *love*, and of a *sound mind*.**
>
> **2 Timothy 1:7**

Why?

That we might serve Him without fear.

Bill Basansky

1
The Search for Reality

There is at least one area where professional people and other highly educated individuals are in total agreement with God: they value their minds very highly.

God also places tremendous value upon man's mind: He made it and He wants man to develop and use it to make his life joyful and successful on this earth.

When God's Word (His Truth) comes into us it makes us free from the bondages of this world and renews our minds to receive the revelation from God. Jesus tells us in His own words,

> **And ye shall know the truth, and the truth shall make you free.**
>
> **John 8:32**

The reason that most people reject and do not believe in Christ Jesus is because their *intellect* has been *unrenewed* and *underdeveloped* in this specific area. They look at the faults of those people who claim to be Christians, and because of darkness, lack of understanding, and just ignorance about God's love or the things of God, they close God out of their lives and reject His Word.

Here is one of the greatest definitions of the word "intelligence." *Intelligence is the ability to adapt successfully to your environment.*

The intellect is very closely related to intelligence and I highly respect intellectual and intelligent people. Being a university professor, I consider myself a professional and an intelligent person.

As a professional person I have to acknowledge that the divorce rate, business failure, alcoholism, drug addiction, mental disorders, etc., are attributed to our inability to adapt successfully to the pressure of a particular environment. The pressures of this world and spiritual wickedness in high places (the works of the devil) are much greater than we are able to cope with in the natural, so we look for a way to escape these pressures through various means such as alcohol, drugs, divorce, suicide, etc.

What we really need is for someone to *illuminate our intellect* and *develop our intelligence* to enable us to successfully accept our responsibilities, adapt to the environment, and release us from the pressures of living. This can only be done by the *One* who created us in His image and likeness, our *Lord* and *Savior Jesus Christ*.

You see, none of us are born intellectual or knowing everything; we must develop our intellect.

If you have questions about your new automobile, you would not go to a plumber for the answers. You would go to the automobile manufacturer himself because he knows every part in that automobile. If you desire to keep your automobile in perfect running condition, then you must follow the manual instructions which are set forth by the manufacturer.

Just because you do not know every part in your automobile doesn't mean that you are stupid or not intelligent. It does mean though, that your mind has not been opened, introduced, renewed, or illuminated in that area.

This is what happens basically, when we reject God. We have not been properly introduced to Him and our intellect and spirit have not been illuminated with His Word. Therefore, I am totally convinced that *it is not the magnitude of man's intelligence that gives him problems* when God begins to talk to him about salvation, healing, prosperity, the baptism in the Holy Spirit, love, joy, peace, etc., but the *lack of development in that particular area*.

I know and wish to tell you that God's Word is real: it carries healing, saving, baptizing, and transforming power today. If you open your heart to Him and ask Him to be the Lord of your life, I guarantee you, on the authority of

God's Word, that He will transform your heart, cleanse you with His blood, and your intellect will be illuminated by the Spirit through the Word of God.

> **If thou shalt confess with thy mouth the Lord Jesus, and shalt believe in thine heart that God hath raised him from the dead, thou shalt be saved.**
>
> **For with the heart man believeth unto righteousness; and with the mouth confession is made unto salvation.**
>
> **Romans 10:9,10**

And Ephesians 4:23,24 tells us.

> **And be renewed in the spirit of your mind;**
>
> **And that ye put on the new man, which after God is created in righteousness and true holiness.**

The world's program today is centered around capturing the mind of God's people scientifically and putting negative thoughts, fear, strife, doubt, and ideas into their minds which are contrary to the Word of God.

Many Christians are struggling today because they do not know when they are being deceived by partaking of and listening to the lies of the devil.

There is a saying that tells us, "If you sleep with a dog, you will have flea bites." People who listen to the lies of the world (the devil) will be oppressed, worried, and tormented by the things of the world.

Many Christians today are having difficulties in their businesses, home life, with their children, marriages, and children are having difficulties in school, etc., because *they have taken their eyes off Jesus* and are being deceived by the lies of the world. As a result, both the reborn Christians and the people who don't know Christ as their Lord and Saviour are lonely, oppressed, fearful, and are searching for reality and truthful answers.

We, as Christians, have been placed in this sinful world to provide an answer for every problem to every needy person. The Word says,

> **But sanctify the Lord God in your hearts: and be ready always to give an answer to every man that**

asketh you a reason of the hope that is in you with meekness and fear.

1 Peter 3:15

Colossians 4:6 says,

Let your speech be alway with grace, seasoned with salt, that ye may know how ye ought to answer every man.

When we know and accept Christ as our Lord and Saviour, we know the answer and the truth to every situation.

Jesus saith unto him, I am the way, the truth, and the life...

John 14:6

The *Truth*, Jesus Christ, dwells within us.

...behold, the kingdom of God is within you.

Luke 17:21

We know that Jesus is the answer for the whole world, and yet some Christians do not know how to cope with the mountain that is before them.

Therefore, what I want to do in this book is to show you how a Christian can live a life of prosperity, divine health, victory, and successful communication with the Almighty God *Who is our source.*

It's true, the world is doing all kinds of things in its search for peace. You can be a millionaire and yet be sick inside, and not have peace because the *Prince of Peace* does not live there.

I tell people that I don't want to be a millionaire, I just want to live like one!

It's not wrong to live like a millionaire, but it's wrong to make the million dollars your god, and to worry about what's going to happen tomorrow.

The world is seeking reality, but Christians *know* the reality. Some, however, are not living the reality. The Christians' problem is not knowing how to use the Word of God to renew their minds. They need to search the scriptures. The Bible says in Hosea 4:6, **My people are destroyed for lack of knowledge.** In other words, *My people live in poverty, sickness, defeat, and perish because they don't know my Word.*

I want to emphasize that I am teaching on the *Power of the Renewed Mind* and how Christians can use the *Power of the Renewed Mind* to live above the problems of the world. There is an answer. If Jesus lived above the problems, and you are the "righteousness of God in Christ Jesus," you have Christ dwelling in you, then shouldn't you and I live above the problems?

The answer is *yes*! But we must learn how to speak to our Heavenly Father and ask. Jesus tells us how to ask in John 16:23,24,

> **And in that day ye shall ask me nothing. Verily, verily, I say unto you, Whatsoever ye shall ask the Father in my name, he will give it you.**
>
> **Hitherto have ye asked nothing in my name: ask, and ye shall receive, that your joy may be full.**

And the Bible tells us in 1 John 5:14,15,

> **And this is the confidence that we have in him, that, if we ask any thing according to his will, he heareth us:**
>
> **And if we know that he hear us, whatsoever we ask, we know that we have the petitions that we desired of him.**

How do we rise above the problems? How do we get this faith that operated in our Lord Jesus Christ to operate in us?

Jesus said in John 14:12,

> **Verily, verily, I say unto you, He that believeth on me, the works that I do shall he do also; and greater works than these shall he do; because I go to my Father.**

Jesus was speaking about you and me. He said, *I give you the power over the devil and all the problems of the world.* Was He telling the truth, or was He lying?

He said, "Even greater things will you do because I go to my Father." Jesus doesn't lie. He never lied, and He never will. He is the Son of the living God, and He tells the truth.

Numbers 23:19 says, **God is not a man that He should lie.** Jesus Christ is Lord and He does not lie. What He said in His Word is just as true today as it was then. In Romans 3:4 He says, **Let God be true, but every man a liar.** I want to have established the fact that Jesus does not lie. His Word does not lie. But every man is a liar. That includes you and me. *Every man is a liar, but God is truth.*

How are we going to come into a relationship with God the Father, whereby we can learn the proper confession, and who we are in Christ Jesus? How can we have the power of God manifest in our lives and through us, so that we can do the things that Christ did? Even greater things, meaning more things.

Here are some of the greater things that will come about. You'll see *more* people being raised from the dead. You'll see *more* people being baptized with the Spirit. You'll see *more* people being saved, because there are more Christians today. That's what Jesus was telling us.

But, in order for these things to come about, you have to have the *power,* and agree and confess the Word of God (Mark 11:23-26).

The *power* is what the Christian in the world needs today. Satan knows this, and he is going to do everything he can to stop you from getting that *power*.

2
Check Your Objectives

Both you as a Christian and Satan, the enemy, know Who is your Source. Satan, the enemy, is going to try to stop you from receiving that *power* to overcome the mountains (Luke 8:12). You need to learn to come against the enemy. One of the first things you need to do is *Check Your Objectives.*

You know about World War II. You may even have been in a war. When there is a war between two nations, what do you supose the weaker nation, or even the stronger one, will try to do to defend itself?

If there were a nation at war against you it would have three major objectives to accomplish against you.

Number 1: If you have a weapon that they are afraid of, then they will do everything within their power to steal it from you, or to keep you from using it. The objective being to stop you from using the weapon on them because they are afraid of it. But, they will not tell you that. They will send all kinds of spies into the camp and try to sabotage everything; they will try to do the things that will deteriorate your strength.

Number 2: The nation will try to cut off your supplies, wanting somehow to cut off the abundant supply that's coming to the front line.

When you see nations fighting and trying to circle the other party, or the enemy, they are trying to cut them off from the mainland, from the main source of their supply. If they can stop the supply, they can take them over with very little fighting or perhaps no fighting at all.

Number 3: The enemy wants to cut the telephone wires. They will try to do everything they can to cut off your communication with the main office. They know that if you have communication with the main office, there will be help coming to you. They are going to do everything they can to destroy communication.

So — what are the enemy's objectives?

Objective Number One: Destroy the weapon that they are afraid of; to blow it up, to dismantle it, to steal it, or to deactivate it.

Objective Number Two: They want to cut off your supply that is coming in to help you fight them.

Objective Number Three: They want to cut off your communications.

I used that example because it is real. You can associate yourself with that. That is what you would do in the natural.

Now, let's take that and put it into the spiritual realm. Here you have on one hand God the Father who loves you, and on the other hand Satan the enemy who wants to destroy you. God the Father has established a means by which we can fight the enemy. He says,

> **For though we walk in the flesh, we do not war after the flesh:**
>
> **(For the weapons of our warfare are not carnal, but mighty through God to the pulling down of strongholds;)**
>
> **Casting down imaginations, and every high thing that exalteth itself against the knowledge of God, and bringing into captivity every thought to the obedience of Christ.**
>
> **2 Corinthians 10:3-5**

If that is so, God has given us a spiritual weapon. And then He says,

> **Beloved, I wish above all things that thou mayest prosper and be in health, even as thy soul prospereth.**
>
> **3 John 2**

As a soldier, if you don't have weapons coming in to you, you are going to deplete in strength. And the objective of the enemy is to cut off the supplies to you, that he may destroy you or take you as his prisoner. I want you to see that the enemy, Satan, is not so dumb. He is *powerful,* he is *mighty,* but he is not *ALL powerful,* and not *ALL mighty.*

There is One mightier than he. His Name is Jesus!

> **Ye are of God, little children, and have overcome them: because greater is he that is in you, than he that is in the world.**
>
> **1 John 4:4**

This Lord Jesus Christ is preparing you and me for a battle. He is saying to you, just as it's real in a war with carnal weapons, so it is with spiritual weapons.

If you desire to be a Christian soldier, strong in the Lord and in the power of His might, then you must,

> **Put on the whole armour of God, that ye may be able to stand against the wiles of the devil.**
>
> **Ephesians 6:11**

3
The Most Powerful Weapon

Satan is going to do everything in his power to try to take away the weapon that the Lord Jesus Christ has provided for us.

What is *The Most Powerful Weapon* against the devil?

It is the powerful Name of Jesus and the Holy Spirit:

> **But the Comforter, which is the Holy Ghost, whom the Father will send in my name, he shall teach you all things, and bring all things to your remembrance, whatsoever I have said unto you.**
>
> **John 14:26**

Psalm 51:11 tells us this:

> **Cast me not away from thy presence; and take not thy holy spirit from me.**

And Paul says in Ephesians 1:13,

> **In whom ye also trusted, after that ye heard the word of truth, the gospel of your salvation: in whom also after that ye believed, ye were sealed with that holy Spirit of promise.**

It is the power of the Holy Spirit working in you that the devil is trying to stop. He will go to any extreme to make you ineffective. He will get into your churches; he will get into your marriage; he will get into your group. He will tell you, "It's not of God." One objective is to stop you from receiving the baptism with the Holy Spirit, with the evidence of speaking in tongues, because Acts 1:8 says that when you receive the baptism with the Holy Spirit, you will receive *power*. The devil knows that if he can keep you from receiving that *power*, he has you licked.

But Jesus is so beautiful. He has prepared and has given you that *power* through the *baptism with the Holy Spirit.*

Jesus wants you to receive the baptism with the Holy Spirit. Jesus wants you to know how to stay healthy physically and spiritually.

As the Lord directs, I will minister to you, through the printed page on the *Renewing of Your Mind,* that you may know who you are in Christ Jesus; what the devil is trying to do; and how you can recognize the devil when he tries to speak to you.

If you are a Spirit-filled Christian you know that the devil has an objective and you should never be up-tight concerning him. You should rejoice that whenever people are talking to you and they say, "Oh, I don't believe in that," you can recognize the influence of the devil. He is using people to speak to you, to try to discourage you, and talk you out of that power.

The baptism with the Holy Spirit is the power that the Bible tells us about in Acts 1:8,

> **But ye shall receive power, after that the Holy Ghost is come upon you: and ye shall be witnesses unto me both in Jerusalem, and in all Judaea, and in Samaria, and unto the uttermost part of the earth.**

Satan is afraid of that power. And you know that he's afraid of it because he will even use people of your church to tell you, "Oh, I don't believe in that. That's not for today." Satan used Peter to rebuke Jesus. But Jesus didn't rebuke Peter. Jesus recognized the spirit that was working through Peter, and He said, **Get thee behind me, Satan** (Matt. 16:23).

Do you know why Jesus recognized the wrong spirit?

Because He had the Spirit of the Father within Him (John 10:30,38). When you know the real Spirit, you too, will recognize the devil. But let me tell you something. Don't be a devil sniffer. Don't go looking for the devil. I'll tell you how to recognize him without any doubt. The Bible says,

But if we walk in the light, as he is in the light, we have fellowship one with another, and the blood of Jesus Christ his Son cleanseth us from all sin.

1 John 1:7

When you are the righteousness of God, then when anything that is not righteousness speaks to you, you'll know that spirit, you'll know that it's the antichrist. That's the devil himself. In John 10:27 Jesus said,

My sheep hear my voice, and I know them, and they follow me.

This tells me that the sheep do recognize the voice of the True Shepherd, just like you and your relative recognize one another's voices.

What I'm saying to you is: when you know Christ deep in your spirit, submit yourself totally to God and you communicate with Him, then you don't have to worry about the devil because the devil will flee from you, your business, your home, your family, and your marriage. But, *you have to know Christ personally as the Source of all your supply.*

The devil will try to keep you from receiving the baptism with the Holy Spirit, because he knows that is one weapon that will destroy him. He knows that you will overpower him, you'll overtake him, and he will no longer have a position in your life, or in your business, because you'll recognize him, and you will take authority over him, and he has to flee.

Submit yourselves therefore to God. Resist the devil, and he will flee from you.

Draw nigh to God, and he will draw nigh to you.

James 4:7,8

Another thing that the devil wants to do is to rob you of your financial blessing. He wants to rob you of your material blessings. He wants to cut off your supply lines so that you will live in poverty, so that you will deny that Christ died for you, and that He was made poor that you might be made rich (2 Cor. 8:9).

You're going to have to recognize that the enemy is at work trying to deprive you of your material blessings.

The Bible says,

Beloved, I wish above all things that thou mayest prosper. . . .

3 John 2

God called you *beloved*. He said, *above all things I want you to prosper*. Bless God! God desires that all His people prosper.

The devil knows that, and he is trying to cut off the line of supply of prosperity by the negative confession out of your mouth. The devil is real! We are in a spiritual battle. It's real. Satan is trying to cut off your supply, make you weak, and make you doubt in a financial area. If the material things aren't coming to you, then you will also doubt in the spiritual area.

Do not confess negatively. Confessing negatively makes God a liar. Then Satan will sit on your shoulder, condemn and laugh at you. You need to be aware that these things are used by the enemy to destroy you.

Don't tell me that you don't want to be blessed by God. Don't tell me that you don't need and want to be healthy. Every person wants to prosper because that's the nature of God. God has instilled it within each person, to be like God. We are prosperous because we are the righteousness of God (2 Cor. 5:17-21; Rom. 8:14-17).

Remember, first, the devil wants to rob you of your weapon. Second, he wants to cut off the supply of the blessing coming to you. And third, he wants to cut off your communications, so you will be cut off from the main source of supply.

Satan is an enemy trying to work on your mind. Everything today that you see — at work, in magazines, every newspaper that you pick up has full pages of advertisement — trying to appeal to your senses: smell, feel, hearing, taste, and sight.

I want you to understand that man is not just *flesh*. I want you to understand that there is more to you than just what you see on the outside. This is the area that we have to learn how to control.

How?

Through the *Power of the Renewed Mind* by the Word of God and the *Holy Spirit*!

4
The Outward Man and the Inward Man

. . .though our outward man perish, yet the inward man is renewed day by day.

2 Corinthians 4:16

If there is an *outward man,* there is also an *inward man.* If there is an inward man, what does he look like? Does he have a mind?

Paul tells us in Ephesians 4:23,24,

And be renewed in the spirit of your mind;

And that ye put on the new man, which after God is created in righteousness and true holiness.

It says in Matthew 17:2,

And was transfigured before them: and his face did shine as the sun, and his raiment was white as the light.

Jesus was transfigured on the mount of Transfiguration, and we know that He looked like this man that we have within us, the *spirit man. This spirit man is real.*

Please read with me, several passages from the Bible. We will resolve several mysteries the world has been trying to put into our minds.

First — it says in 1 Corinthians, chapter 15, beginning with verse 38,

But God giveth it a body as it hath pleased him, and to every seed his own body.

Every seed has its own body. Even the grapes are different from tomatoes. Potatoes are different from barley and from wheat. Corn is different from watermelons. Every seed has its own body.

If that is true, then birds are different from pigs; pigs are different from dogs; dogs are different from fish; fish are different from cows, and man is different from monkeys.

Let's read verse 39,

> **All flesh is not the same flesh: but there is one kind of flesh of men, another flesh of beasts, another of fishes, and another of birds.**

The Bible says that a man is made after the image and likeness of God. Genesis 1:24,25 tells us this,

> **And God said, Let the earth bring forth the living creature after his kind, cattle, and creeping thing, and beast of the earth after his kind: and it was so.**
>
> **And God made the beast of the earth after his kind, and cattle after their kind, and every thing that creepeth upon the earth after his kind: and God saw that it was good.**

You see, God made fish; God made birds; God made animals; God made the beast after its own kind, but then in verse 26,

> **And God said, Let us make man in our image, after our likeness....**

If I am in an *image and likeness of God,* my first question is, "God what do you look like?"

And God, being so beautiful will answer your question if you are sincere. If you want to know, read in John 4:24,

> **God is a Spirit: and they that worship him must worship him in spirit and in truth.**

That means *speaking in spiritual language,* because God is Spirit.

In John 3:6, He says,

> **That which is born of the flesh is flesh; and that which is born of the spirit is spirit.**

Therefore, flesh speaks to flesh, and spirit speaks to the spirit. So, you see the difference between the fleshly (carnal) and the spiritual language.

Now, God said He made us in His image and likeness, and I said, ''Well, God, what do you look like?''

He said, ''Well, I'm the Spirit.''

''Do you have a body?''

''Yes, I have a body.''

''Well, show me your body. What do you look like?''

He said, ''Well, turn to Matthew 17:2, and you'll see my Son, Jesus, and when you see my Son you will see me.''

> **I and my Father are one.**
>
> **John 10:30**

> **...he that hath seen me hath seen the Father; and how sayest thou then, Shew us the Father?**
>
> **John 14:9**

Bless God! I don't have to look any further. Matthew told us that Jesus was transfigured, and when He was transfigured, Elijah was there, and Moses was there, and in the fifth verse, God the Father, straight from a cloud said,

> **...This is my beloved Son, in whom I am well pleased; hear ye him.**

God said He made you and me from the beginning. We look like we look because we look like God, and God looks like we do in the inner man: like Father like son (John 14:9-11). When God made us His eternal breath was blown into an inanimate object. That inanimate object, the body, couldn't do anything but just lie there. For example: my ear cannot tell me what to do. My nose cannot tell me when to eat. My foot cannot tell me when to go to sleep. This is an inanimate thing, it doesn't think for itself.

But, there is something that dwells in us that thinks for itself. I want you to see that *God created something to communicate with Him.* He created *you* — not to sit in church like a tombstone. He made us to be as *lively stones.* He made you to rejoice, and to clap your hands, and to dance before God. *He created you* and *me* that *we may have communication, or communion with God* — that we may walk and talk in the ''cool of the day'' with God the Father.

When God made this shell that we call the body, He did not make the spirit to fit the body. *Listen to me!* He made the body to fit the spirit (Heb. 10:5). God the Father made you and me in His image, and He put a body over that spirit. Therefore, there is a spirit man that dwells within this body that's as tall as I am. There is a spirit man that has fingers, has a mind, eyes, ears, mouth, and feet. He has everything that you see that your physical body has.

There is an inward man and an outward man.

5
Feed the Spirit Man

There is no problem with God to heal the body. I don't care how sick it may be, or how deteriorated. You see, there is no difficulty with God to heal you, but there is something you must do. You have to accept the fact with your mind, that God does and will heal, when you let your *spirit* mind and your *natural mind* be one.

The Bible says,

> **But he that is joined unto the Lord is one spirit.**
> **1 Corinthians 6:17**

In other words, when you are one, then you are joined to the Lord of one spirit. The mind and the spirit become one with God. Then He will say, "My ways are your ways, and my thoughts are your thoughts," but until such time, there is no way that we can think like God because the *natural mind rebels against God.* Romans 8:6-8 tells us,

> **For to be carnally minded is death; but to be spiritually minded is life and peace.**
>
> **Because the carnal mind is enmity against God: for it is not subject to the law of God, neither indeed can be.**
>
> **So then they that are in the flesh cannot please God.**

We read in Galatians 5:16,17,

> **This I say then, Walk in the Spirit, and ye shall not fulfil the lust of the flesh.**
>
> **For the flesh lusteth against the Spirit, and the Spirit against the flesh: and these are contrary the one to the other: so that ye cannot do the things that ye would.**

So God then made the *body,* and He already had the *spirit,* and the *body fit the spirit.*

Let me illustrate it another way. You have gone to a store and bought yourself a pair of gloves. Now, when you went into the store, did you buy the gloves without trying them on? If you did, and when you got home you may have found that they were the wrong size, and you had to take them back to the store. The smart thing to do is to go to the store, and put your hand into the glove, and when the glove fits the hand, then you buy the glove. You see, your hand was not made for the glove, the glove was made for the hand.

Now, do you mean to tell me that your glove tells you when to put it on, and when not to put it on? Do you mean to tell me that your glove knows what time of the day it is?

Any person knows that a glove doesn't tell you what to do. You tell a glove what to do as you put your hand in the glove, and wherever the hand goes, the glove follows.

Do you see what we need to do?

It should be the *spirit* telling your *body* where to go, how to be healthy, when to sleep, and when to eat, instead of your body telling your spirit what to do. Too many Christians have given their bodies priority over the spirit. The spirit has to be fed with spiritual food.

Let me ask you another question. Have you eaten this week?

I'll answer the question for you. Of course, you have. You eat because you need the fuel for your boy to be strong and to function properly. If you didn't eat, you would lose weight, you would lose strength, and you would die.

If that is true in the natural — and food is necessary for your physical body, I ask you, how are you feeding your spirit man? Think about that. How are you feeding your spirit man?

Some people are big physically, but very thin spiritually. The spirit man is so thin that you have to look with a magnifying glass to find him, because he has not been fed.

The Bible says,

> **That which is born of the flesh is flesh; and that which is born of the Spirit is spirit.**
>
> **John 3:6**

You are going to have to feed the flesh with food that the flesh desires, and you will also have to feed the spirit with spiritual food. And spiritual food can only come from the Spirit Himself, who is our God, who is our Father, who is our Source of supply.

You see, here we have a situation where we have a spirit man, and a carnal man. If you are going to feed the carnal man, you are going to have to feed the spiritual man also.

How?

With spiritual food.

Let's read 1 Corinthians 15:44,

> **It is sown a natural body; it is raised a spiritual body. There is a natural body, and there is a spiritual body.**

That is what I've been telling you; there is a natural body, and there is a spiritual body. If there is a natural body, you must feed it and take care of it. If there is a spiritual body, then it must be taken care of spiritually.

In verses 42 and 43 of the same chapter, it says,

> **So also is the resurrection of the dead. It is sown in corruption; it is raised in incorruption:**
>
> **It is sown in dishonour; it is raised in glory: it is sown in weakness; it is raised in power.**

You see, we have these seeds. They are the bodies. When we die to self, the weakness dies with us, and we are raised up in a spiritual body, and this spiritual body is strong. Then, the Bible tells us that we can do all things through Christ Jesus, because we put on a new man.

In other words, when your spirit is born from above, it becomes alive — we say a *born again experience.* When we are in the world, our bodies are alive; spiritually we are dead. But, when we are born again, our spirit becomes alive. When God took the inanimate object, that clay, and blew His breath into it, the two came together, and out of that was produced a brand new life that we call the living soul.

By the same token, when a man and wife join in a union, they produce a child, which is a brand new life. But it takes two of them. So, God is speaking to us in this fashion.

We are going to have to get saved; be *born again.* Then our spirit, joined with God's Spirit, indwells this temple, the body.

6

That Ye Henceforth Walk

> **This I say therefore, and testify in the Lord, that ye henceforth walk not as other Gentiles walk, in the vanity of their mind.**
>
> **Ephesians 4:17**

The Bible speaks in the above verse about the mind. He is speaking to you, and to me, to born again Christians. He says, "Don't walk in the vanity of the mind as other Gentiles."

You see, the "other Gentiles" *don't know what they can have in Christ Jesus.* They don't know that they can have *all things through Christ.* They don't know that they can have the *power or the righteousness of God.* They live in a negative, dark world. But you have been delivered from the *powers of darkness,* and you have been *translated into the kingdom of His dear Son.* Your sins are forgiven, you have been washed with the blood, and now you are *the righteousness of God!*

Therefore, he says, "Don't walk with your mind like the rest of the Gentiles that don't know Christ and the power thereof." He is talking to you and me about our minds. He goes on to say in verse 18:

> **Having the understanding darkened, being alienated from the life of God through the ignorance that is in them, because of the blindness of their heart.**

You see, we can be alienated or pushed away, separated from God by the devil if we don't look to God's Word. If you become a Christian and don't follow through in God's Word, if you don't make an effort to receive what God has for you, Satan will put doubts in your mind. Satan will attempt to cut off the supply line that is coming from

God, to rob you of the blessings that you are entitled to receive.

Do you see that?

The Bible is telling us that we need to be alert and *press on towards the mark of the high calling in Christ Jesus* (Phil. 3:14).

In Ephesians 4:19 he says,

> **Who being past feeling have given themselves over unto lasciviousness, to work all uncleanness with greediness.**

I want you to see that the *uncleanness of greediness* here is of the world, and not for Christians.

Verses 20-22 say,

> **But ye have not so learned Christ;**
>
> **If so be that ye have heard him, and you have been taught by him, as the truth is in Jesus:**
>
> **That ye put off concerning the former conversation the old man....**

I want you to read slowly so that it may sink into your spirit. It says, *that ye put off concerning the former conversation.* He is speaking to you about communication, about talking, about conversation. He says, ''the old man.'' The old man is the personality of the individual who has been in rebellion against God. That you put away all that — the old man of the world. Then he continues in verses 22,23:

> **...which is corrupt according to the deceitful lusts;**
>
> **And be renewed in the spirit of your mind.**

Here, the Bible is telling you that your spirit and your mind have to be renewed. And that you put on the new man, which after God is created in righteousness and true holiness.

How?

He tells us in 2 Corinthians 5:17:

> **Therefore if any man be in Christ, he is a new creature: old things are passed away; behold, all things are become new.**

He is telling us to be renewed in the spirit of our mind, and that we put on a new man, which after God is created in righteousness and true holiness.

Because we have righteousness and true holiness through Christ Jesus we can come boldly unto the throne of grace in the time of need. You see, 2 Corinthians 5:20,21 tells us,

> **Now then we are ambassadors for Christ, as though God did beseech you by us: we pray you in Christ's stead, be ye reconciled to God.**
>
> **For he hath made him to be sin for us, who knew no sin; that we might be made the righteousness of God in him.**

So, here the Scripture says that we have been made the righteousness of God, and *because we are the righteousness of God in Christ Jesus, our minds have to be renewed.* The Bible is saying to us as Christians, "Don't think like the world does. Don't worry about the oil. Don't worry about the gas. Don't worry about the 'rapture.' Because Jesus said, 'I am the Great *I AM.* I am the *Rapture* and the *Resurrection.'* Jesus is more than enough."

He says in Deuteronomy 8:16, **Who fed thee in the wilderness with manna?** And let me tell you, God has not lost His recipe for manna. If He fed them, He will feed you today and tomorrow. God says His cattle are still doing well on the hill. He says the hills are His, the mountains are His, and the cattle thereof. If He fed Elijah by the brook with bread and meat twice a day, bless God, He'll do it for you! What's good enough for Elijah is good enough for you and me! God didn't love him any more than He loves me or vice versa.

> **For there is no respect of persons with God.**
>
> **Romans 2:11**

God says, "Don't think like the world. They say, "Where is my food going to come from?"

> **Therefore I say unto you, Take no thought for your life, what ye shall eat, or what ye shall drink; nor yet**

for your body, what ye shall put on. Is not the life more than meat, and the body more than raiment?

Behold the fowls of the air: for they sow not, neither do they reap, nor gather into barns; yet your heavenly Father feedeth them. Are ye not much better than they?

Which of you by taking thought can add one cubit unto his stature?

And why take ye thought for raiment? Consider the lilies of the field, how they grow; they toil not, neither do they spin:

And yet I say unto you, That even Solomon in all his glory was not arrayed like one of these.

Wherefore, if God so clothe the grass of the field, which to day is, and to morrow is cast into the oven, shall he not much more clothe you, O ye of little faith?

Therefore take no thought, saying, What shall we eat? or, What shall we drink? or, Wherewithal shall we be clothed?

(For after all these things do the Gentiles seek:) for your heavenly Father knoweth that ye have need of all these things.

But seek ye first the kingdom of God, and his righteousness; and all these things shall be added unto you.

Take therefore no thought for the morrow: for the morrow shall take thought for the things of itself. Sufficient unto the day is the evil thereof.

Matthew 6:25-34

He says, "You believe my Word. I am the same. I change not." (Mal. 3:6.)

I want you to see that I'm speaking about the *flesh*. I'm not speaking about the *spirit man.* I had to bring that in so that you may understand. I am talking about the *natural man* and the *natural mind.*

The Word of God says in Romans 8:5,

For they that are after the flesh do mind the things of the flesh; but they that *are after the Spirit the things of the Spirit.*

When you desire God you will do the things that God would have you to do. But if you are after the things of the world your mind is not on God. God says that those who think about the world will get the things of the world. But they that are after the Spirit will get the things of the Spirit.

That is not to say you shouldn't care for your body or for your family. We need to have these things, but when it comes to the point of being so carnally minded or materially minded that your farm, or your money, or your business becomes your god, then you are serving the wrong god. God said,

Thou shalt have none other gods before me.
Deuteronomy 5:7

This is where you have to be careful. Riches or wealth aren't wrong. God wants you to be prosperous. But don't ever make riches your god.

When the rich man came to Jesus, Jesus told him to "sell everything and follow me." And he couldn't do it. Then, Jesus said it would be easier for a camel to go through the eye of a needle than for a rich man to go to heaven. Here is where the apostles said, "Well, Lord, what about us?" This shows me that they were prosperous fishermen. And let me tell you, Peter, James, John, and the rest of them, when they went out fishing and caught all those fish, I'm sure they had a place where they sold them. They didn't eat all those fish themselves. And because they sold the fish, that meant that they were pretty wealthy, for Peter said, "It's all right for you to be wealthy as long as you don't make money your god."

The Bible says in Romans 8:6-8:

For to be carnally minded is death; but to be spiritually minded is life and peace.

Because the carnal mind is enmity against God: for it is not subject to the law of God, neither indeed can be.

So then they that are in the flesh cannot please God.

I want you to understand that the carnal mind is an enemy of God. *Because the carnal mind is at enmity, hostile against God.* The carnal mind wants to fight God all the time. It doesn't want to accept the fact that we can speak the *word of faith* and disease will die and sickness will depart from our bodies (Mark 11:24-26).

I went with a friend of mine to his farm where the bugs were killing his crops. We prayed, and as we lifted the leaves from the maize and cotton, those green bugs were everywhere — but they were dead, scores of them — dead!

You see, in the natural mind you could never perceive that. Those bugs were all over the plants on his next-door-neighbor's farm, and the plants were dying. And yet — my friend's plants were growing beautifully green; the bugs were dying and falling to the ground.

Bless God! God can take any situation and make something for you! Even the bugs that fell to the ground, God made fertilizer out of them.

You are going to have to *believe in the spirit and confess with your mouth.* With the natural eye, man will say, ''Those bugs will eat my crop.'' But with the *spiritual eye,* he will say, ''Bless God, they are dead. The bugs are God's concern, and God will take care of them — because we are not under the curse, but under grace!

Hallelujah! *The battle is His, but the victory is ours*!''

7
Led by the Spirit

For as many as are led by the Spirit of God, they are the sons of God.

Romans 8:14

If you are led by the Spirit of God, the Spirit of God speaks to your spirit. This is very important, because the Word says, *if they that are led communicate with Him, there is all knowledge, all power, all supply.* If you can communicate with Him then you are His son. It doesn't matter who you are; whether you are female or male, the Spirit of God is master in you; you are a son of God.

We just read, "For as many (they) that are led by the Spirit of God, they are the sons of God (you are His son)." If you are His son, truly are His son, then you know everything that God the Father would have you to do and know. He says in Romans 8:16,

The Spirit itself beareth witness with our spirit, that we are the children of God.

Now, how can the Spirit of God bear witness with our spirit?

The first thing we must do is become a spiritual child of God. To have the inheritance that God has promised us we have to be born again.

After you are a born again Christian you are going to have to learn to speak to the Father. The only perfect way that you can speak to the Father is with the heavenly language.

When you speak in a heavenly language to the Father, the Father speaks to your spirit through His Spirit. His Spirit — the Holy Spirit — dwells within your body.

Proverbs 20:27 says,

The spirit of man is the candle of the Lord, searching all the inward parts of the belly.

Where does the spirit dwell?

Within your belly.

He says,

He that believeth on me, as the scripture hath said, out of his belly shall flow rivers of living water.

(But this spake he of the Spirit, which they that believe on him should receive: for the Holy Ghost was not yet given; because Jesus was not yet glorified.)

John 7:38,39

God doesn't speak through your mind, into your mind. He speaks into your spirit that's born again. When God speaks to the spirit, the Spirit of God brings the thought into your mind, and then you know that God is speaking to you.

How do you know whether God tells you something or if it is the enemy, because they are both spirits?

By the fruit ye shall know. Your thoughts have to line up with the Word of God and vice versa.

The Bible says in Philippians 4:8,9,

Finally, brethren, whatsoever things are true, whatsoever things are honest, whatsoever things are just, whatsoever things are pure, whatsoever things are lovely, whatsoever things are of good report; if there be any virtue, and if there be any praise, think on these things.

Those things, which ye have both learned, and received, and heard, and seen in me, do: and the God of peace shall be with you.

He says think about these things — if there be any virtue — think about them, then you know that it's the Spirit of God.

If the Spirit of God tells you to do something for a brother, don't blame the devil just beause you don't feel like it or it's not the right time of the year. If God says for you to give something to your brother, or for you to go and pray for him, or to love him, or help him with his work in his business, and you obey God, then you're in the family of God, and God is loving them and meeting their immediate needs through you. It's not the devil; it's the *Holy Spirit* telling you. So listen to the Spirit of God, obey and help with your time, talents, and money. Christians ought not get involved over their heads and support organizations that do not propagate the Gospel, because it's an abomination to God. The breath of God will become a curse and a punishment to you and to me, if we misuse God's money, time, and talents.

For she did not know that I gave her corn, and wine, and oil, and multiplied her silver and gold, which they prepared for Baal.

Therefore will I return, and take away my corn in the time thereof, and my wine in the season thereof, and will recover my wool and my flax given to cover her nakedness.

Hosea 2:8,9

It says in Romans 8:16,17:

The Spirit itself beareth witness with our spirit, that we are the children of God:

And if children, then heirs; heirs of God, and joint-heirs with Christ. . . ."

We are joint-heirs with Christ Jesus.

It says in 1 Corinthains 6:17,

But he that is joined unto the Lord is one spirit.

If Christ is led by the Spirit of the Father, and you are led by the Spirit of the Father, He is saying to us, "They that are joined unto the Lord are of one spirit." We are one spirit. If we are one spirit, then we have the authority, the same authority that God the Father gave Jesus our Lord.

Do you see that?

It's not what you think or how you feel; it's what the *Word of God* says. If the Word of God says you're rich, bless God, you're rich. If the Word of God says you're saved, you are saved.

The Bible says the Word is powerful in every way, but we have to get the *Word of God into* our spirits to have this power, making our minds as the mind of Christ.

The Word of God is saying to you and to me, that we are of one spirit, if 1 Corinthians 6:17 is true, ''But he that is joined unto the Lord is one spirit.'' Then he says in Philippians 2:5,

> **Let this mind be in you, which was also in Christ Jesus.**

If we put on the mind of Christ, and if we are led by the Spirit of God, then whatever Jesus thinks, we should think. Whatever Jesus knows, we should know. Whatever Jesus does, we should do. How He speaks we should speak. Anything He does we should do like Him in every way. And our minds have to be such that we will always look to God the Father as our Source, because He loves us as much as He loves Jesus (John 17:23; 1 John 4:17).

You will never receive anything unless *you pray through Jesus to God the Father* and ask according to His will. That's what Jesus said to His disciples: ''When you pray, pray like this, Our Father who art in heaven.''

If you and I are going to ask God anything, we ask God the Father in the Name of Jesus. For He says, ''No man comes unto the Father except through Jesus Christ.''

You pray a perfect prayer in the spirit, in a heavenly language. Romans 8:26 says,

> **. . . for we know not what we should pray for as we ought: but the Spirit itself maketh intercession for us with groanings which cannot be uttered.**

He tells us to *pray in the Spirit,* and when we pray in the spirit, *our spirits know how to pray.*

This is what God is saying to you and to me,

> **Fulfil ye my joy, that ye be likeminded. . .**
>
> **Philippians 2:2**

Likeminded, like who?

Well, like Jesus, that's who. He is saying, "Fulfill ye my joy; you will fulfill my joy when you will obey my *Word*, your mind will be the mind of Christ, and you will walk and talk prosperity and health, and you will confess everything that I have given to you in my *Word*."

He is saying, "Be ye likeminded — my greatest joy is for you to be like Christ Jesus." And then He says, "Having the same love, being of one accord, or one mind." He is saying that we are going to have to be of one mind, of one accord with Christ Jesus. We need to renew our minds to the point that our mind will be full of the Lord. He says,

> **Thou wilt keep him in perfect peace, whose mind is stayed on thee: because he trusteth in thee.**
>
> **Isaiah 26:3**

When we let our minds drift somewhere else, when we're not thinking about the Lord, we aren't keeping our eyes upon Him, then we cannot be and are not in perfect peace. That's why many Christians today are suffering from unrenewed minds.

How can Christians have the mind of Christ?

> **Seek ye the Lord while he may be found, call ye upon him while he is near:**
>
> **Let the wicked forsake his way, and the unrighteous man his thoughts: and let him return unto the Lord, and he will have mercy upon him; and to our God, for he will abundantly pardon.**
>
> **For my thoughts are not your thoughts, neither are your ways my ways, saith the Lord.**
>
> **Isaiah 55:6-8**

I want you to see that when your thoughts are not the thoughts of God, the Bible says unrighteous thoughts, like those of unrighteous men, you should forsake them. Don't be like the world, don't think negative thoughts, but think positive.

When we return unto the Lord, He will abundantly pardon.

When you turn away from the Lord, when you confess doubt and unrighteous thoughts of unbelief, even though you're a Christian, (when those thoughts come from *you)* you are committing sin (Rom. 14:23).

You can keep from committing that sin. When a thought comes in and does not stay, and you do not dwell upon it, and you don't speak it from your mouth, that thought will be stillborn. It will die and never come into existence. You must rebuke that thought, and claim your righteousness, and who you are in Christ Jesus. It will die and never come about. As you claim that, that thought that went through your mind died, and you committed no sin. But if you start to dwell upon those negative thoughts, when you start to worry about your crops not making it, that your finances are not coming in; when you start dwelling upon that, it will surely come to pass. You have allowed the negative thought to go into your heart.

> **...out of the abundance of the heart the mouth speaketh.**
>
> **Matthew 12:34**

Here is what you must do. Rebuke those thoughts, don't be like the world, don't think negative: think positive. Say, "I am free from poverty, sickness, and disease."

> **And ye shall know the truth, and the truth shall make you free.**
>
> **They answered him, We be Abraham's seed, and were never in bondage to any man: how sayest thou, Ye shall be made free?**
>
> **Jesus answered them, Verily, verily, I say unto you, Whosoever committeth sin is the servant of sin.**
>
> **And the servant abideth not in the house for ever: but the Son abideth for ever.**
>
> **If the Son therefore shall make you free, ye shall be free indeed.**
>
> **John 8:32-36**

Say, "I am the righteousness of God. God wants me to prosper. God wants me to be in good health, and God wants me to *communicate with Him in a heavenly language."* When you know who the Supplier is, when you know your weapon, and when you know how to communicate with the Supplier, the devil has no chance with you.

In Isaiah 59:7 He says, "**. . . their thoughts are thoughts of iniquity. . . .**" The reason God's thoughts are different and higher than the negative thoughts of the unrighteous man is that thoughts of the unrighteous man are thoughts of iniquity, but God's thoughts are perfect thoughts.

That's why He said, **. . . no man speaking by the Spirit of God calleth Jesus accursed. . .** (1 Cor. 12:3).

You see, when you are saved and baptized with the Holy Spirit, your mind becomes one with Him. When your mind becomes like the mind of Christ and you become one in spirit, He says, "They that are led by the Spirit of God are the sons of God."

When you're a son of God, then He says, "But they that are joined unto the Lod are of one spirit." We are a son of God. We are of one spirit. Then He says, "Let this mind be in you which is in Christ Jesus."

Remember, He told us in Philippians 4:8, that if there be any virtue or good report, or anything lovely, think about these things. Jesus does not think of you as being bad. He doesn't think of you as being stupid. He doesn't think of you as being dumb. He thinks of you as a beautiful child of God, bought with a price. *The price of His shed blood.*

You are the righteousness of God. The Bible tells us in 1 Corinthians 1:30 that we are His wisdom because He dwells in us. We have all the wisdom that we need because Christ dwells within us.

If that is true, then you and I ought to have victory in every area. But so often we don't obey the Word, especially the commandments of God.

> **. . . if ye shall hearken diligently unto my commandments which I command you this day, to love the Lord your God, and to serve him with all your heart and with all your soul.**
>
> **Deuteronomy 11:13**

In Mark 12:30,31 we read,

> **And thou shalt love the Lord thy God will all thy heart, and with all thy soul, and with all thy mind, and with all thy strength: this is the first commandment.**
>
> **And the second is like, namely this, Thou shalt love thy neighbor as thyself. There is none other commandment greater than these.**

Your mind is the thing that you have the most difficulty with. He says that when you can love Him with your mind, when you can *Renew Your Mind with the Word of God;* when you totally love God, then you'll totally love your husband or your wife. But your first obligation is to love God, because **God so loved the world that He gave his only begotten Son...** (John 3:16). That was for us. We have fellowship with God the Father through our Lord Jesus Christ.

> **...Return unto me, and I will return unto you, saith the Lord of hosts....**
>
> **Malachi 3:7**

God is pleading for Christians to renew their minds. God is calling you and me to return to Him so He may return to us, and give us a victorious life in Christ Jesus through the *power of our renewed minds.*

To contact the author,
write:
Bill Basansky
Love and Grace Fellowship
P. O. Box 7126
Fort Myers, Florida 33911

Please include your prayer requests and comments when you write.

Additional copies are available at your local bookstore or by writing:

Harrison House
P. O. Box 35035 • Tulsa, OK 74153

In Canada, contact:

Word Alive
P. O. Box 284
Niverville, Manitoba
CANADA ROA 1EO

For international sales in Europe, contact:

Harrison House Europe
Belruptstrasse 42 A
A — 6900 Bregenz
AUSTRIA

The Harrison House Vision

Proclaiming the truth and the power
Of the Gospel of Jesus Christ
With excellence;

Challenging Christians to
Live victoriously,
Grow spiritually,
Know God intimately